PRIMARY SOURCE
EXPLORERS

A JOURNEY WITH SIEUR DE LA SALLE

LISA L. OWENS

LERNER PUBLICATIONS ◆ MINNEAPOLIS

Content consultant: David Nichols, PhD, University of Kentucky, Associate Professor of History, Indiana State University

Lerner Publications Company
A division of Lerner Publishing Group, Inc.
241 First Avenue North
Minneapolis, MN 55401 USA

For reading levels and more information, look up this title at www.lernerbooks.com.

Main body text set in AvenirLTPro 12/18.
Typeface provided by Linotype AG.

Library of Congress Cataloging-in-Publication Data

Names: Owens, L. L., author.
Title: A journey with Sieur de La Salle / Lisa L. Owens.
Description: Minneapolis : Lerner Publications, [2016] | Series: Primary
   source explorers | Includes bibliographical references and index. |
   Audience: Ages 8–11.
Identifiers: LCCN 2016006414 (print) | LCCN 2016007033 (ebook) | ISBN
   9781512407754 (lb : alk. paper) | ISBN 9781512411003 (eb pdf)
Subjects: LCSH: La Salle, Robert Cavelier, sieur de, 1643–1687—Juvenile
   literature. | Explorers—North America—Biography—Juvenile literature.
   | Explorers—France—Biography—Juvenile literature. | Canada—
   History—To 1763 (New France)—Juvenile literature. | Mississippi River
   Valley—Discovery and exploration—French—Juvenile literature.
Classification: LCC F1030.5 .O94 2016 (print) | LCC F1030.5 (ebook) | DDC
   910.92 [B] —dc23

LC record available at https://lccn.loc.gov/2016006414

Manufactured in the United States of America
1-39347-21159-11/17/2016

CONTENTS

 = Denotes primary source

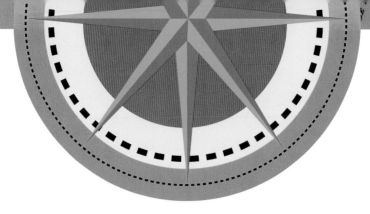

INTRODUCTION
A LOST HISTORY

French explorer Sieur de La Salle lived during the seventeenth century near the end of the Age of Exploration. This was a time when Europeans explored and colonized parts of what they called the New World. La Salle explored the Great Lakes region, the Mississippi River, and the Gulf of Mexico. He is probably best known for giving the Louisiana territory its name.

Biographer Francis Parkman wrote that La Salle "kept journals and made maps" of his expeditions. These journals and maps are examples of primary sources—information created by those who witnessed an event. Historians use primary

This engraving of Sieur de La Salle was created in the nineteenth century, long after La Salle died. It is not considered a primary source.

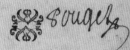

JOURNAL
HISTORIQUE
DU DERNIER VOYAGE
que feuM. de laSale fit dans le Golfe de
Mexique, pour trouver l'embouchure,
& le cours de la Riviere de *Miſſicipi*,
nommée à preſent la Riviere de Saint
Loüis, qui traverſe la LOUISIANE.

Où l'on voit l'Hiſtoire tragique de ſa mort, &
pluſieurs choſes curieuſes du nouveau monde.
Par Monſieur *JOUTEL*, l'un des Com
pagnons de ce Voyage, redigé & mis en ordi
par Monſieur *DE MICHEL*.

A PARIS,
Chez ESTIENNE ROBINOT, Libraire,
Quay & attenant la Porte des Grands
Auguſtins, à l'Ange Gardien.

MDCCXIII.
Avec Approbation & Privilege du Roy.

sources to understand and describe historical people, places, and events. Some of La Salle's letters survived. But most of his other personal records were lost. Other maps and firsthand accounts as well as artworks and objects from his ships still exist, though. These items fill in some of the blanks in La Salle's life and help us better understand—and more accurately report on—his role in history.

A seventeenth-century engraving shows the city of Rouen at the edge of the Seine River.

CHAPTER 1
SIEUR DE LA SALLE'S EARLY DAYS

La Salle was born into a Roman Catholic family in 1643 in Rouen. Rouen was the capital of Normandy, France. His parents were Catherine Geest and Jean Cavelier. Cavelier was a rich trader and landowner. La Salle had several siblings, including an older brother named Jean. La Salle's name at birth was René-Robert Cavelier. Due to his family's wealthy status, he would gain the title Sieur de La Salle as an adult. It means "gentleman from La Salle." La Salle was his family's estate near Rouen.

As a boy, La Salle attended a school run by the Jesuits, members of a Catholic religious order. He took lessons in

This seventeenth-century colored engraving depicts a Jesuit priest working with young children in France.

astronomy, math, languages, mapmaking, and religion. He planned to become a priest. He was a good student and took vows to start his training as a priest at the age of seventeen.

But he became restless. By the age of twenty-two, La Salle had a change of heart about being a priest. He'd read about explorers traveling to distant lands. He wanted to take part in such adventures. La Salle wanted to make his own way in the New World like the French explorers Samuel de Champlain and Jean Nicolet. So he left the Jesuit order. In 1666 he sailed across the Atlantic Ocean for New France, a French colony in North America. The colony covered parts of modern Canada and the Great Lakes region.

Soon La Salle arrived in Montreal and met up with his brother Jean, who had become a Sulpician priest. The Sulpician order helped found Montreal. Jean had moved there about a year before. His mission was to convert First Nations peoples to Christianity.

A seventeenth-century oil painting of King Louis XIV as a young boy

MEETING THE KING

France's King Louis XIV had reigned since just before La Salle was born. Louis XIV took the throne after his father died in the spring of 1643. He was just four years old then. So his mother and godfather took over the king's official duties. This gave Louis a chance to grow up and prepare for his important role.

When La Salle was about six, his family saw the young king in person. Louis XIV—now a boy of eleven—visited Rouen with his mother. La Salle was part of the crowd greeting the royal carriages and king's guard as they passed through town. This was the first of several encounters La Salle would have with the king of France.

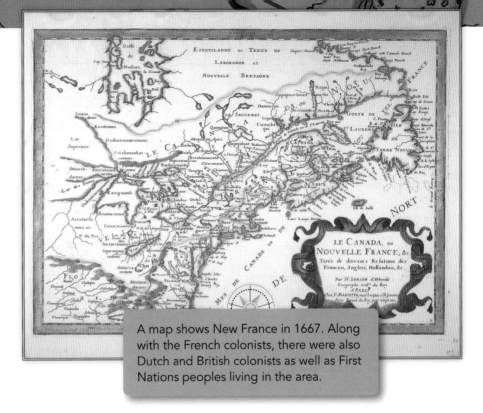

A map shows New France in 1667. Along with the French colonists, there were also Dutch and British colonists as well as First Nations peoples living in the area.

La Salle hoped to become involved in new explorations. But first, he had to earn a living. He had arrived in New France with very little money. So Jean used his connections to help La Salle get a land grant from the governor. The grant included land along the Saint Lawrence River. La Salle's new job was to help settle the area.

WHAT DO YOU THINK?

Why might La Salle's brother Jean and other missionaries have wanted to teach their religious beliefs to other cultures? Why do you think this work was important to them?

This image, created in the 1880s, shows the Lachine settlement. The building beside the flag was La Salle's home.

CHAPTER 2
LAUNCHING AN EXPEDITION

Over the next few years, La Salle cleared his land. He farmed some of it and set aside plots for other Europeans to buy. He started what became a thriving fur-trading post too. All this activity attracted more newcomers. The settlement was known as Lachine, which means "China." Many believe the name refers to La Salle's dream of traveling to China.

Colonists worked together to build homes and create a community at Lachine. During this time, La Salle became rich. He also learned many new skills he'd never needed in France. To survive, he had to be able to hunt, find his way through the wilderness, and help protect the settlement from enemy attacks.

La Salle enjoyed founding Lachine. But by 1669, he was ready to move on. He'd heard that there might be an all-water route through North America to China. He wanted to be the one to find it. It would help expand French business interests in the New World. This could make him famous, and trading with China would make him even richer than he already was. La Salle believed he'd find this route by exploring the Ohio and Mississippi Rivers. He thought they might lead to China by way of the Gulf of California into the Pacific Ocean. But first, he had to raise the money to pay for the trip.

La Salle asked the French government for permission to lead his expedition. He asked for financial help too. Daniel de Rémy de Courcelle was the governor of New France. He agreed to La Salle's plan. But he wouldn't give him the money. La Salle would have to pay for the trip himself. The governor also insisted La Salle travel with a group of Sulpician missionaries. They had already been approved for their own journey to Canada's Outaouais region in present-day western Quebec. That group wanted to convert more Native peoples to Christianity.

Determined to explore, La Salle accepted the governor's terms. The two groups would travel together as far as Lake Ontario. La Salle sold all his property, bought supplies for the trip, and hired men to go with him. The expedition of twenty-four men and seven canoes left Lachine on July 6, 1669.

A missionary priest on the trip described the group's travel conditions: "Your lodging is as extraordinary as your vessels; for, after paddling or carrying the canoes all day, you find mother earth ready to receive your wearied body. If the weather is fair

Beaver pelts, such as these, were popular trading goods in New France.

LEARNING THE LANGUAGE

To create a successful fur-trading post, La Salle had to work with local First Nations peoples. They were experts at hunting and trapping beavers. Beaver pelts and skins were used to make blankets, hats, and other goods. La Salle studied indigenous languages so he could communicate and do business with the Native peoples. The Seneca Indians he befriended told him of the Ohio, which means "beautiful water," and the Messi-Sipi, or "big water." La Salle eventually decided to explore these waterways.

you make a fire and lie down to sleep without further trouble; but, if it rains, you must peel bark from the trees, and make a shed by laying it on a frame of sticks."

The priest also noted that their meals often consisted of Indian corn with meat. He said, "This sort of life seemed so strange to us that we all felt the effects of it; and before we were a hundred leagues [300 miles, or 483 kilometers] from Montreal, not one of us was free from some malady or other." La Salle's voyage was off to its exciting yet difficult start.

WHAT DO YOU THINK?

Why do you think the governor of New France refused to pay for La Salle's expedition?

When La Salle's expedition encountered Seneca Indians in Irondequoit Bay, the two groups exchanged gifts including food such as Indian corn, shown here.

CHAPTER 3
ADJUSTING TO LIFE AS AN EXPLORER

By August 1669, La Salle's expedition had made it to the head of the Saint Lawrence River. Then they followed Lake Ontario to reach Irondequoit Bay, near present-day Rochester, New York.

There they met some Seneca Indians. Interpreters helped the groups communicate. Both wanted a peaceful relationship. And the Seneca proudly hosted the Frenchmen. In his journal, missionary priest René Bréhant de Galinée wrote about exchanging gifts with them: "We had no sooner arrived in this place than we were visited by a number of Indians, who came to make us small presents of Indian corn, pumpkins, blackberries, and whortleberries—fruits of which they had an abundance. We

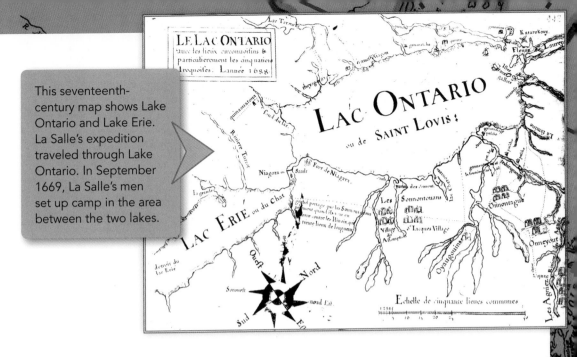

This seventeenth-century map shows Lake Ontario and Lake Erie. La Salle's expedition traveled through Lake Ontario. In September 1669, La Salle's men set up camp in the area between the two lakes.

made presents in return, of knives, awls, needles, glass beads, and other articles which they prize." Both the French and Native peoples believed gifts were a sign of peace and friendship.

After several days, La Salle's group continued their journey by water to present-day Hamilton, Ontario. They arrived in September 1669. Here they learned they were getting closer to the Ohio River. This was an important milestone. La Salle still hoped this river would lead to finding a water route to China.

At this point, the missionaries decided to leave the expedition and keep moving west. Because the weather was turning colder, La Salle and his men set up camp for the winter. They would start the next leg of their journey in the spring.

Exactly what happened next is hard to know for sure. Up to this point in the journey, historians can find details written by members of the missionary group. After the two groups split up, the missionary writings contain only guesses and secondhand accounts of where La Salle's men may have gone.

A SUCCESS STORY

The plaque in Fairport Harbor, Ohio, seems to accept the story of La Salle traveling on the Ohio River to Louisville. Here's the full text on the plaque:

> In search of a westward-flowing river, French explorer and trader René-Robert Cavelier, Sieur de La Salle (1643–1687) mounted an inland expedition from the south shore of Lake Erie at the mouth of the Grand River in the fall of 1669. Thought to be the first European to see the Ohio River, La Salle journeyed up the Grand River and portaged to a tributary of the Ohio; from there he descended as far as the falls at Louisville, Kentucky. La Salle's explorations both expanded the fur trade and helped to consolidate French claims to the Mississippi River valley. French dominance in Ohio ended following British victory in the French and Indian War (1754–1763).

Many researchers say that La Salle himself claimed to have navigated the Ohio River. Yet most of La Salle's own records were destroyed. So many existing sources from that time rely on other reports of what La Salle said and did. Some say La Salle's expedition traveled south on the Ohio to present-day Louisville, Kentucky. They say his crew deserted him there to return to Canada. Others say La Salle never reached the Ohio River. And still other scholars say that maybe he reached it alone and that his crew had abandoned him earlier.

However the end of that expedition happened, it is clear that La Salle did not find a route to China. He didn't even reach the Pacific Ocean. And by about 1671, he was back in Montreal. He had run out of money and needed to find a new venture to occupy his time.

WHAT DO YOU THINK?

Why do you think there are so many different opinions about the outcome of La Salle's first expedition? What details would make you trust one source over another?

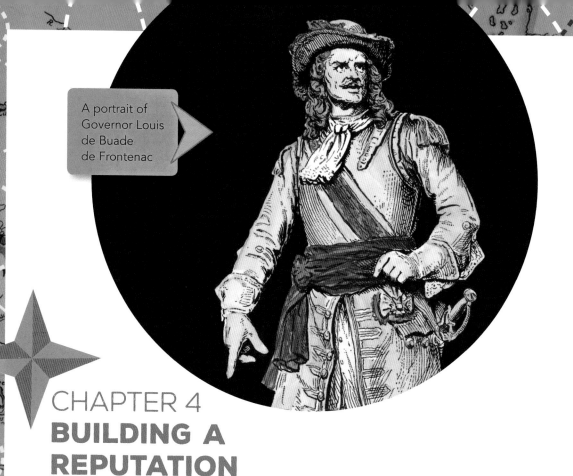

A portrait of Governor Louis de Buade de Frontenac

CHAPTER 4
BUILDING A REPUTATION

La Salle soon met New France's new governor, Louis de Buade de Frontenac. The governor asked for La Salle's help. He was impressed with La Salle's knowledge of the fur trade. He wanted La Salle to build a new fort and trading post. It would be on Lake Ontario in present-day Kingston, Ontario. The governor hoped to gain control over access to the fur available in the region.

La Salle completed Fort Frontenac in 1673. It was made from earth and wood. Then he sailed to France in 1674 to ask to be made commander of the fort. He also asked for noble status. He felt he deserved it for his work as an explorer for France.

A seventeenth-century oil painting shows the front of the Palace of Versailles.

Frontenac sent a letter of recommendation for King Louis XIV to consider. He wrote that La Salle was "more capable than anybody else I know here to accomplish every kind of enterprise and discovery which may be entrusted to him, as he has the most perfect knowledge of the state of this country, as you will see, if you [will] give him a few moments of audience."

At the Palace of Versailles, La Salle made a good impression on the king's court. In the winter of 1674–1675, he met with King Louis XIV. Louis XIV agreed to make La Salle the commander of Fort Frontenac and grant him noble status. But La Salle had to do the following:

This 1685 image shows Fort Frontenac near Lake Ontario.

FORT IN THE CATARAQUI

Fort Frontenac was built on the Saint Lawrence River. The river connects with Lake Ontario. It was originally called the Cataraqui, which is the French version of an indigenous word. It means "muddy river," "place of retreat," and also "impregnable."

- rebuild Fort Frontenac in stone
- open the land surrounding the fort to settlers
- build a church
- pay for everything himself

La Salle was happy to make this deal. Commanding the fort and establishing its trading post would benefit France. It would also make him rich again. This would give him the freedom to go on more expeditions. He wanted to do more exploring.

This report was written by La Salle in 1674, about his visit with King Louis XIV.

Family and friends were excited by La Salle's connection to the king. And they supported La Salle in his new role. They helped get him started by lending him money. La Salle and his men spent the next two years rebuilding the fort in stone. They added a mill, a bakery, and sleeping lodges. They also put cannons into the walls that surrounded the fort. They turned Fort Frontenac into a busy and profitable trading post.

A twentieth-century painting by J. D. Kelly shows La Salle inspecting the stone construction of Fort Frontenac in 1676. This painting is not a primary source, but Kelly is known for painting well-researched images of important events in Canadian history.

Not everyone thought highly of La Salle. He often kept to himself. Some under his command claimed that he was hard to work for and that he used unfair trading practices. He agreed he was a tough leader. But he said he was only harsh when his men made serious mistakes. He did not tolerate bad behavior or a lack of order.

WHAT DO YOU THINK?

Some of La Salle's men thought he was too strict. La Salle felt that that was true only when his men behaved badly. Can both of these points of view be accurate? How might you go about deciding?

A twentieth-century illustration shows La Salle meeting with King Louis XIV, asking for permission to explore the Mississippi River.

CHAPTER 5
EXPLORING FOR THE CROWN

In 1678 La Salle prepared for a new adventure. King Louis XIV gave him permission to pursue plans to claim the Mississippi River territory for France. Again, La Salle would have to pay for the expedition. As before, he was able to raise the money through loans from friends and relatives. He set to work finding men and supplies.

This time, he joined forces with Henri de Tonti, an Italian soldier, explorer, and fur trader. Tonti had lost his right hand in battle. He had a metal hook that replaced it. He was known as Iron Hand. Tonti became La Salle's second in command, and in August 1679, their thirty-two-member crew set sail

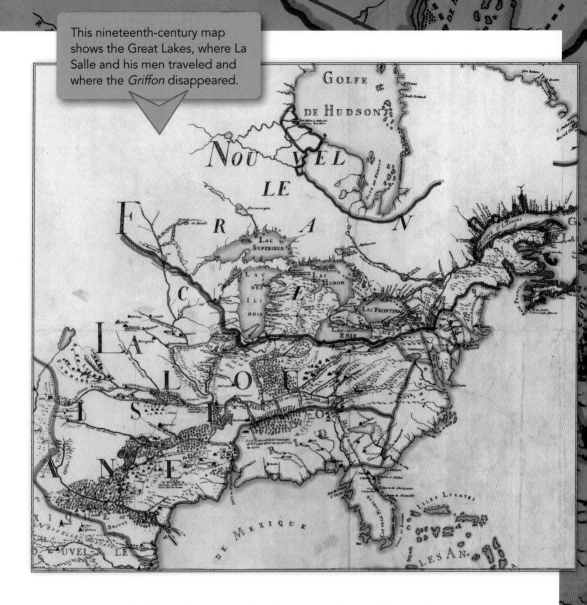

This nineteenth-century map shows the Great Lakes, where La Salle and his men traveled and where the *Griffon* disappeared.

on the *Griffon*. This was the first wooden sailing ship on the Great Lakes.

They traveled across the Great Lakes, stocking the ship with furs bought along the route. At Green Bay, La Salle sent a small crew to Niagara to sell the furs. They were supposed to return to Green Bay. But they were never heard from again. The *Griffon*, along with her cargo and crew, had disappeared.

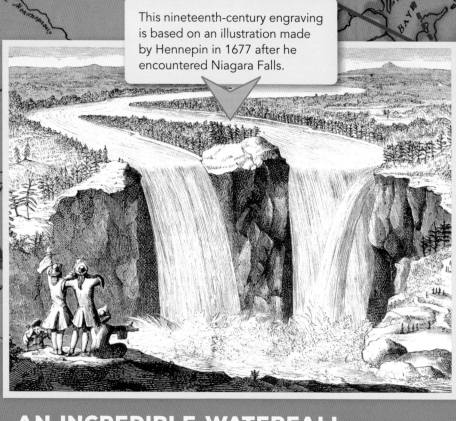

This nineteenth-century engraving is based on an illustration made by Hennepin in 1677 after he encountered Niagara Falls.

AN INCREDIBLE WATERFALL

Father Louis Hennepin, a member of La Salle's second expedition, was the first European to see Niagara Falls. He was part of a crew La Salle sent there to build a fort and a ship. On seeing the falls for the first time, Hennepin wrote: "We entered the beautiful river Niagara, which no bark had ever yet entered. . . . There is an incredible [waterfall], which has no equal." He described the rapid waters and the strong current: "It hurries down all the animals which try to cross it without a single one being able to withstand its current. They plunge down a height of more than five hundred feet [152 meters], and its fall is composed of two sheets of water and a cascade, with an island sloping down. In the middle these waters foam and boil in a fearful manner."

One of the men who traveled with La Salle, Father Louis Hennepin, illustrated the *Griffon* in a book about his explorations called *Nouvelle Decouverte d'un tres Grand Pays, situé dans l'Amerique* (A New Discovery of a Vast Country in America) in 1697.

One explanation could be that the ship sank in Lake Michigan during a storm. Another possibility is that the crew stole the goods and sank the ship before running away. Some have wondered if the *Griffon* traveled outside Lake Michigan and sank in another waterway, such as the Straits of Mackinac or Lake Huron. The mystery surrounding the disappearance has persisted for more than three hundred years. People still hunt for the wreckage.

WHAT DO YOU THINK?

Why do you think people are still interested in finding the *Griffon*'s wreckage?

While waiting for the *Griffon*'s return, the expedition needed shelter. They built Fort Miami in January 1680 at the mouth of the Saint Joseph River in Michigan. At the end of the year, they established the settlement at Fort Crevecoeur near present-day Peoria, Illinois.

La Salle's 1682 expedition is probably the one he's best known for. A report by one of his men notes that La Salle "began with his ordinary activity and vast mind, to make all preparations for his departure." He organized a group of fifty-four Frenchmen, Native peoples, women, and children. The group traveled in canoes on the Illinois River down to the Mississippi River. They arrived near present-day Saint Louis in February and reached the Gulf of Mexico on April 9, 1682.

This nineteenth-century painting depicts La Salle's journey down the Mississippi River with a fleet of canoes.

LA SALLE'S EXPEDITION 1679–1682

Once ashore near the mouth of the Mississippi, La Salle posted a cross and the French coat of arms. La Salle and his men sang a hymn and then shouted "Vive le roi!" (Long live the king!). Then, with all his men as witnesses, La Salle claimed the region for France and King Louis XIV. Native peoples who were present "responded with loud applause and cries." They seemed to enjoy the ceremony, but they did not understand La Salle's words.

The region La Salle claimed included the Mississippi River and all the land connected to waters that fed into it. He named this territory Louisiana to honor King Louis XIV. The region belonged to France until 1763 when it was given to Great Britain and Spain. Then, in 1803, the Louisiana Purchase transferred it to the United States.

La Salle's final expedition was arranged by King Louis XIV. La Salle left France in July 1684, setting sail for North America. He had four ships and several hundred settlers and soldiers. They planned to establish a French colony in Louisiana at the mouth of the Mississippi River on the Gulf of Mexico.

This nineteenth-century painting depicts La Salle's arrival at the mouth of the Mississippi River. The painting is one of several depicting La Salle's journey, painted by American artist George Catlin.

A twentieth-century illustration shows La Salle claiming Louisiana for France.

LOUISIANA LAND CLAIM

"I, this ninth day of April, one thousand six hundred and eighty-two, in virtue of the commission of His Majesty . . . have taken, and now do take, in the name of his Majesty . . . possession of this country of Louisiana, the seas, harbors, ports, bays, adjacent straits, and all the nations, peoples, provinces, cities, towns, villages, mines, minerals, fisheries, streams, and rivers within the extent of the said Louisiana."

—Sieur de La Salle

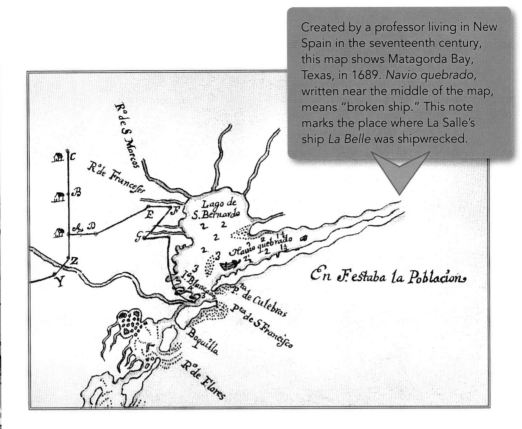

Created by a professor living in New Spain in the seventeenth century, this map shows Matagorda Bay, Texas, in 1689. *Navio quebrado*, written near the middle of the map, means "broken ship." This note marks the place where La Salle's ship *La Belle* was shipwrecked.

Before sailing, La Salle wrote to his mother at Rouen: "At last, after having waited a long time for a favorable wind, and having had a great many difficulties to overcome, we are setting sail. . . . We all have good hope of a happy success." He closed his letter by thanking his mother for her support and asking her not to worry.

The expedition suffered many problems. There was a shipwreck, and another ship was seized by pirates. Many crew members died, and the crew was unhappy with La Salle's leadership. They were especially upset by his failure to find the Mississippi. He'd missed the mouth of the river. Instead, they landed at Matagorda Bay, in present-day Texas.

On March 19, 1687, five crew members attacked La Salle. One of those men blamed his brother's death on La Salle's carelessness. The man shot and killed La Salle near present-day Navasota, Texas. An expedition member who saw the event said the murderer "killed him outright with one shot in the forehead and then returned to join the group" as if nothing had happened. La Salle was forty-three years old when he died.

A seventeenth-century engraving depicts the murder of La Salle.

The Murther of Mons.ʳ de la Salle

M. Vander Gucht Sculp:

TIMELINE

- **1643** La Salle is born in November.

- **1650** A young La Salle first crosses paths with France's King Louis XIV.

- **1666** La Salle resigns from his Jesuit training.

  La Salle founds Lachine, a settlement in New France.

- **1669** La Salle leads an expedition in search of a water route to China.

- **1673** La Salle builds Fort Frontenac.

- **1674** La Salle travels to France to request royal appointments.

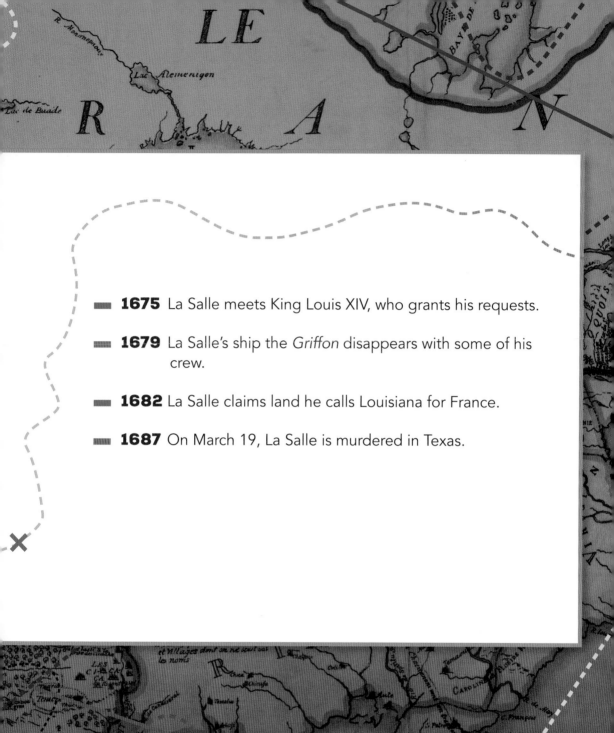

1675 La Salle meets King Louis XIV, who grants his requests.

1679 La Salle's ship the *Griffon* disappears with some of his crew.

1682 La Salle claims land he calls Louisiana for France.

1687 On March 19, La Salle is murdered in Texas.

SOURCE NOTES

4 Francis Parkman, *La Salle and the Discovery of the Great West: France and England in North America, Part Third* (Boston: Little, Brown, 1908), Kindle edition, 662.

11,13 Ibid., 556.

13 Ibid., 561.

14–14 Orsamus H. Marshall, "The First Visit of De La Salle to the Senecas, Made in 1669 [Microform]: Read before the Buffalo Historical Society, March 16, 1874," 16, available online at Internet Archive, accessed August 2016, https://archive.org/details/cihm_28603.

16 Ohio Historical Markers: La Salle Expedition 1669 (20–43), Waymarking.com, accessed August 2016, http://bit.ly/2aJvmYm.

19 Parkman, *La Salle*, 1734.

28 John Upton Terrell, *La Salle: The Life and Times of an Explorer* (New York: Weybright and Talley, 1968), 179.

29 Ibid., 185.

32 Parkman, *La Salle*, 5320.

33 "Rene Robert Cavalier: La Salle's Final Journey," Mariner's Museum, accessed August 2016, http://bit.ly/2aJH7hD.

31 Daniel Spurr, *River of Forgotten Days: A Journey Down the Mississippi in Search of La Salle* (New York: Henry Holt, 1998), 220.

26 Frank H. Severance, *Studies of the Niagara Frontier* (Buffalo: Buffalo Historical Society, 1911), 315.

GLOSSARY

colonist: one who moves to live in a new territory that is controlled by a foreign government

convert: to change another person's religious beliefs

expedition: a journey by a group of people who want to explore a distant land, or the group of people exploring a new land

First Nations: the official term in Canada for the nations of indigenous peoples

indigenous: descended from or belonging to the original occupants of a land before the land was taken over by others

malady: a disease or illness

missionary: a person who goes to a foreign country to do religious work

New World: the Western Hemisphere, including North and South America

noble: part of the upper class

Sulpician: a member of the French Society of Saint-Sulpice, whose main role was to train priests and do community work

SELECTED BIBLIOGRAPHY

Bruseth, James E., and Toni S. Turner. *From a Watery Grave: The Discovery and Excavation of La Salle's Shipwreck*, La Belle. College Station: Texas A & M University Press, 2005.

Cox, I. J., ed. *The Journeys of La Salle and His Companions: 1668–1687, as Related by Himself and His Followers, Tonty, Hennepin, Joutel, etc.*, Vol. 2. New York: Williams Barker, 1906.

Joutel, Henri. *The La Salle Expedition to Texas: The Journal of Henri Joutel 1684–1687*. Edited by William C. Foster. Austin: Texas State Historical Association, 1998.

Parkman, Francis. *La Salle and the Discovery of the Great West: France and England in North America, Part Third*. Boston: Little, Brown, 1908.

Severance, Frank H. *Studies of the Niagara Frontier*. Buffalo: Buffalo Historical Society, 1911.

FURTHER INFORMATION

France in America: Chronology
http://international.loc.gov/intldl/fiahtml/fiachronology.html
This helpful chart tracks France's history with America from the sixteenth century to the beginning of the nineteenth century.

Kuligowski, Stephanie. *La Salle: Early Texas Explorer*. Huntington Beach, CA: Teacher Created Materials, 2012. Learn more about La Salle and his explorations across North America.

Louis XIV
http://www.history.com/topics/louis-xiv
This article provides biographical information about King Louis XIV.

Pelleschi, Andrea. *Samuel de Champlain*. New York: PowerKids, 2013. Read this book to learn about one of the explorers who inspired Sieur de La Salle.

Waxman, Laura Hamilton. *A Journey with Henry Hudson*. Minneapolis: Lerner Publications, 2018. Read all about another explorer who longed to sail to Asia.

LERNER
SOURCE

Expand learning beyond the printed book. Download free, complementary educational resources for this book from our website, www.lerneresource.com.

INDEX

PHOTO ACKNOWLEDGMENTS

The images in this book are used with the permission of: Library of Congress, map background, p. 25; Sarin Images/Granger, NYC, p. 4; Library of Congress (F1030.5.J86), p. 5; © Tallandier/Bridgeman Images, p. 6; © Bibliotheque Les Fontaines, Chantilly, France/Archives Charmet/Bridgeman Images, p. 7; © Château de Versailles, France/Bridgeman Images, p. 8; The W. H. Pugsley Collection of Early Canadian Maps/McGill University, p. 9; Queen's University/University of Toronto Libraries, p. 10; © Heeb Christian/Prisma Bildagentur AG/Alamy, p. 12; © iStockphoto.com/Starcevic, p. 14; University of Toronto Map and Data Library, p. 15; © Jason Chapek, p. 16; DEA/G. Dagli Orti/The Granger Collection, New York, p. 19; © North Wind Picture Archives/Alamy, p. 18; Archives nationales de France/Wikimedia Commons (PD), p. 20; Centre des archives d'outre-mer, courtesy of Library and Archives Canada, p. 21; painting by J. D. Kelly/Library and Archives Canada (LAC C-007962), p. 22; © Private Collection/Bridgeman Images, p. 24; © Private Collection/Ken Welsh/Bridgeman Images, p. 26; Wikimedia Commons (PD), pp. 27, 32; courtesy of the Paul Mellon Collection/National Gallery of Art, Washington DC, p. 28; © Laura Westlund/Independent Picture Service, p. 29; © De Agostini Picture Library/Bridgeman Images, p. 30; © The Stapleton Collection/Bridgeman Images, p. 31; The Granger Collection, New York, p. 33.

Cover: © North Wind Picture Archives/Alamy (main); Library of Congress (map).